Userbayeva Feruza

Today's interpretation of Sadriddin Aini's activities

© Userbayeva Feruza
Today's interpretation of Sadriddin Aini's activities
by: Userbayeva Feruza
Edition: September '2024
Publisher:
Taemeer Publications LLC (Michigan, USA / Hyderabad, India)

ISBN 978-93-5872-456-1

© **Userbayeva Feruza**

Book	:	Today's interpretation of Sadriddin Aini's activities
Author	:	Userbayeva Feruza
Publisher	:	Taemeer Publications
Year	:	'2024
Pages	:	46
Title Design	:	*Taemeer Web Design*

Userbayeva Feruza History course student
Chirchik State Pedagogical University

2024 Chirchik

Introduction

After our country gained independence, great work was done in all aspects of social and political life: self-awareness, deep understanding of spiritual and educational values and education of young people in the spirit of love for the Motherland and the people. Special programs developed by the government with long-term goals have become crucial in improving spiritual life. The education of talented young people, sending them to the world's most advanced higher educational institutions, has become a matter of state importance. The pedagogues of Jadid also considered the issue of youth education as a matter of life or death. In this sense, one can feel a strange similarity and closeness in the educational-spiritual and socio-political life of the beginning and end of the 20th century. The cornerstone method of the Jadid movement is the Jadid schools. This opinion is unanimously recognized by historians. The original goal of this movement was to promote the identity of the nation, fundamentally reform the socio-political system, and the independence of the nation and the homeland. It is known that only the new generation can make such great changes. For this, it is necessary to raise a generation that is in step with developed nations. The traditional local schools, which educated great world thinkers such as Farobi, Beruni, Ibn Sina, Ulugbek, Navoi, were completely cut off from world development from the 16th century, moreover, they were in a state of disarray due to the colonial system. it was not possible. Therefore, radical reform of local schools, establishment of schools and higher educational institutions that can meet the requirements of the times became the primary and main task of modern thinkers. Modern pedagogues raised the issue of restoring elementary schools based on the method of "usuli savtiya" ("sound method") to the level of state policy: they created elementary alphabets, textbooks on specific subjects, reading books.

The main part

The ideals of modernism and the priorities of modernist ideas The term Jadid appeared in Turkish Turks for the first time during the reign of Sultan Selim III (1739-1802). Abubakr Ratib Effendi, who was sent as an ambassador to Austria, explains the administrative system he saw there as Nizomi jaded in his reports to the Shah. The new system built after the French Revolution of 1789 was called the French Charter. In those years, Nizomi Jaded envisaged the Europeanization of the military system in the narrow sense, and the modernization of science, education, industry and agriculture in the broad sense. Therefore, the term jadid was used as a concept that expresses supporters of innovation, ideas of innovation. At the end of the 19th century, huge cultural-educational, socio-political changes, new relations in the world civilization began to enter the lands of Turkestan, albeit slowly in one way or another. In the words of Abdulla Awlani, supporters of news are called mullahs who leak newspapers. At this point, it is permissible to quote the following thoughts of Islam Karimov, we imagine the future of our country not in our small shell, but in a deep reduction of universal and democratic values. We see our perspective in liberalizing state and social governance, introducing human rights and freedoms, and diversity of opinions into our lives, using the experience of developed countries. We are supporters of peaceful, free and prosperous life and mutually beneficial cooperation with the whole enlightened world and the international community. One of the main factors of the quality and effectiveness of higher education is the relevance of science and education. The combination of science and education is effective in three ways, as we discussed above. In particular, it is desirable to form a certain scientific focus on the topic of organization and management of the emergence of the Jadidist movement in Turkestan. One of the first and main steps to ensure the realization of requirements for level, quality and efficiency is the fact that training organization is left alone and convenient.

One of the main aspects that increases the quality of education and determines the level of the teacher is the constant awareness of the science teacher about the scientific news on the subject. It is necessary for the teacher to constantly familiarize himself with new scientific literature, articles published in scientific journals and other scientific publications on the subject of the history of Uzbekistan. It is also required to get acquainted with scientific-popular publications, historical-artistic publications and materials published in the mass media on the subject. In general, the relevance of science and education as an important factor of modern development is the study, study and promotion of every topic in the history of Uzbekistan. is one of the most basic requirements. Independence is considered a great historical event in the history of our country, and this historical process freed our people from long-lasting dependence and colonialism. As stated by the first President I. Karimov, another example of this is the work of our ancestors who raised the idea of marifat during the Tsar colonial period. Mahmudhoja Behbudi, Munavvarqori, Abdurashidkhanov, Abdulla Avloni, Ishaqkhan Ibrat, Abdurauf Fitrat, Abdulla Qadiri, Abdulhamid Cholpon, Usman Nasir, hundreds of philanthropists, selfless people, etc. . The modernists, whose main goal is to reform the educational system in Turkestan, are concerned with the problems of getting out of economic and political dependence, who can defend the interests of national independence, and realized that there should be personnel with modern knowledge. Jadids dreamed of raising the cultural level of the nation to international level, and for this they believed that it is necessary to educate young people in the best educational institutions of Europe. Mahmudhoja Behbudi wrote in Oyna magazine about the influx of young people from abroad and benefiting his country as follows: Children and students should be sent to Makkah, Medina, Egypt, Istanbul and Russia's dorilfun and dorils to cultivate religious, secular and modern people.

It is known that Munavvarqori Abdurashidkhanov also showed courage in this way. His aid organization Jamiyati Khairiya "directed aid work for students who were secretly sent to Turkey, Orinburg, Ufa and Azerbaijan after graduating from primary schools." In the literature written during the Soviet period, modernism is described as "bourgeois-liberal movement".

After the collapse of the SSR, the name of the Jadidist movement and its representatives was revived. Historians, literary experts, linguists, philosophers, lawyers, art historians and pedagogues have achieved preliminary results in the study of the scientific and literary heritage of the past. In the years of independence, the works of Fitrat, Cholpon, Abdulla Avloni in 2 volumes, Behbudi, Abdulla Qadiri, Sidkiy Khandayliqi, Ibrat, Ajziy, Sofizoda in 1 volume, as well as the works of Fayzulla Khojayev, Munavvarqori, Polvonniyoz Haji Yusupov were published. 20 famous representatives of Jadids are included „Unforgettable figures. The album-book "Representatives of the Jadidchilik movement" (Tashkent, 1999) was published. Their work was included in textbooks and manuals. On September 16-18, 1999, an international conference was held in Tashkent on the topic "Central Asia at the beginning of the 20th century:

reforms, renewal, development and struggle for independence (modernism, autonomy, independence)", in which the USA, Germany, France, Italy, the Netherlands, Eminent scientists from Turkey, Russia, India and other countries exchanged views with their Uzbek colleagues on the latest conclusions collected in world science about modernism and independence movements. It was recognized that the Jadidic movement is a phenomenon of global importance. At the conference, an international scientific council was formed to study this problem. Jadidism used to function as a movement in the field of culture. The representatives of this movement called for struggle for development, development of Turkic languages, enrichment of literature in these languages, study of secular sciences, use of scientific achievements, and equality of women and men. Later, Jadidists propagated the ideas of pan-Turkism. The representatives of the Jadid movement often called themselves progressives, later Jadids. The advanced progressive forces of that time, first of all, the intellectuals, felt that the local population was lagging behind the global development and understood the need to reform the society. Jadidism was essentially a political movement. It has periods of formation and defeat, which can be conditionally divided into four.

In Turkestan, Bukhara and Khiva, these periods are 1895-1905; 1906-1916; 1917-1920; Includes the years 1921-1929. In the first period, Tsarist Russia firmly established itself in Turkestan. With the help of his political agents (representatives), he not only restricts the powers of local khans and emirs, but also turns them into puppets, creates conditions for Russian and Western investors to work and live, and looks after the interests of various companies and joint-stock companies. At the same time, the demands and needs of the local population were not taken into account, disregard for their religious beliefs, customs, and their disdain increased. Judges with a high academic and life level were replaced by inexperienced people, bribery and social-political injustice escalated. Literature plays an important role in the development of any country. Because in addition to spiritual food for the people, lessons from the past, and an invitation to a bright future, today's problems are reflected in it. Intellectuals who understood the power of literature looked for ways to use it effectively and influence people. There are great literary representatives of each era, whose works involuntarily embody the breath of that era, the social, economic and, of course, political situation of that era. In the history of our country, there are many intellectuals who are enlightened, thirst for knowledge and intend to educate the future generation as well. First of all, they were eager to acquire knowledge, then spread it to the people around them, especially children, to improve educational processes, and to create perfect textbooks. Especially at a time when they invaded our country and plundered its wealth, they left an indelible mark in the history of our country by showing the right path to the youth and inviting them to acquire the most advanced knowledge of their time. In particular, those who left a good legacy in terms of opening a school for children, developing and implementing new pedagogical methods. Because education is the real foundation of the future. The political and social changes taking place in the life of the world and our country did not leave the intelligentsia indifferent. They united under one goal and began the work of restoring the spiritual wealth of our people, accepting modern educational programs and applying them to educational processes. The manifestations of this movement went down in history as a

Jadidist movement. Jadidism is based on modernism. Jadid means new. There was a time when the socio-political aspects of Jadidism were not discussed. However, the autonomy of Turkestan, which lasted for 72 days, is the biggest and most beautiful event in history. And at the same time, the most tragic, blood-soaked incident. After that, Cholpon wrote a poem "To the broken country".

We can say that "Jadidlar set 9 main directions. The first of them was independence. We gained independence 32 years ago. The next issue was to identify and introduce the minority to the world. This is not a 1-2 year or reform event. Therefore, this is one of the important issues that they have left. Or rather, the introduction of the Uzbek language on a global scale was seen as an important development. Jadids dreamed that writers on the level of Alisher Navoi would grow up. That is why Qadiri, Behbudi, Fitrat,

Cholpon wrote great and beautiful works. In my opinion, the path started by the ancients will continue. The historian says that their noble and noble intentions will come true one day. Of course, on the basis of ancient goyas, very large goyas have been embodied. Even today, historians continue to apply the ideas based on these ideas. After our country gained independence, great work was done in all aspects of social and political life: self-awareness, deep understanding of spiritual and educational values and education of young people in the spirit of love for the Motherland and the people. Special programs developed by the government with long-term goals have become crucial in improving spiritual life. The education of especially talented young people, sending them to the world's advanced higher education institutions, has become one of the issues of state importance. The pedagogues of Jadid also considered the issue of youth education as a matter of life or death. In this sense, one can feel a strange similarity and closeness in the educational-spiritual and socio-political life of the beginning and end of the 20th century.

The cornerstone method of the Jadid movement is the Jadid schools. This opinion is unanimously recognized by historians. The original goal of this movement was to promote the identity of the nation, fundamentally reform the socio-political system, and the independence of the nation and the homeland. It is known that only the new generation can make such great changes. For this, it is necessary to raise a generation that is in step with developed nations. The traditional local schools, which educated great world thinkers such as Farobi, Beruni, Ibn Sina, Ulugbek, Navoi, were completely cut off from world development from the 16th century, moreover, they were in a state of disarray due to the colonial system. it was not possible. Therefore, radical reform of local schools, establishment of schools and higher educational institutions that can meet the requirements of the times became the primary and main task of modern thinkers. Modern pedagogues raised the issue of restoring elementary schools based on the method of "usuli savtiya" ("sound method") to the level of state policy: they created elementary alphabets, textbooks on specific subjects, reading books. The administrators of the governorate overcame the opposition of the bigoted clerics and trained teachers who could meet the requirements of the time. Such activities of theirs took place in the process of intense struggles, persecutions and pressures. But despite this, their activities continued. In particular, such pages can be seen in Sadriddiy Aini's life.

We know that Sadriddin Ainiy is a writer, scientist and public figure of Uzbek and Tajik literature of the 20th century. Ainiy carried out research work in Uzbek and Tajik literature as a historian, literary critic and scientist. He wrote novels about poets and scientists such as Rudaki, ibn Sina, Sa'di, Wasifi, Bedil, Navoi, Ahmed Donish. He was born in 1878 in the village of Soktari, Gijduvan district, Bukhara region. His father was a mill foreman, and his grandfather was a mullah. At the age of six, his father sent Sadriddin to a school near the mosque. However, the school teacher was illiterate, so the father took his son from this school and placed him in the school for women of Bibi Khalifa, the wife of the village mullah. In school education, he learns to read and write. Syed Akbar, who was educated in Bukhara, made a great contribution to the development of literacy. Sadriddin Ainiy experienced various periods and events in his life. The first period of his life was the Emirate period, the feudal medieval period and the beginning of capitalist relations, and the next period was the period of struggle to destroy the old system and establish a new socialist society. Consequently, these two periods are widely reflected in Sadriddin Aini's work. For example, a certain development of the picture of life of that time or the beginning of a new movement in Bukhara can be an example of this. In the second half of the 19th century, supporters of the emirate did not want any changes. Ahmad Makhdumi Donish (1826-1897), the ancestor of the Tajik people and the founder of the educational movement during the Bukhara Emirate regime. , according to the words of Master Ainyi, 'shines bright and shining ... like the morning star that appears at the end of dark nights'. This noble man awakened a number of intellectuals of Bukhara to a new life with his work, especially the famous work "Nawadir ul-Waqe". Ustoz Ainiy is considered one of those awakened ones.

Ustoz Aini's impressions from the reading are very rich and meaningful.

About Ahmadi Donish's work "Nawadir ul waqae", Sadriddin Aini wrote the following thoughts: I read this book again and again, "I enjoyed it a lot... After that I understood why Ahmad-Makhdum was called an infidel." In this book, he ruthlessly criticized the official mullahs, he fearlessly wrote about the corruption between the ummah and the scholars, the flaws in the educational methods, the valuelessness and unnecessaryness of many things taught in madrasas. That's why they called him an infidel! After that, I got to know who Ahmad-Makhdum was, and my attitude towards mullahs and the lessons I studied changed; writes down his thoughts. It can be seen that Sadriddin Ainiy read and commented on this work with special attention to its interpretation. He said that he had specially researched whether this work was written according to the truth and expressed his thoughts and opinions in this regard. In short, reading this book has changed my way of thinking." That is, "...Our view, continues Sadriddin Aini, about emirs, ministers, mullahs and their lives. "That day almost completely changed." This change is considered as knowing the truth of the situation of the people of Bukhara Emirate and looking for ways to correct them. At the end of the 19th century and especially at the beginning of the 20th century, the Emirate of Bukhara could not stay out of the world news. Various newspapers came to Bukhara and published materials related to various world events. In particular, on the initiative of Ismail Gaspary (1851-1914), one of the main leaders of the Tatar modernist movement, in 1883-1914, the "Tarjimon" newspaper published in Tatar language was distributed in Bogchasaray. Magazines "Habl-ul-matin" published in Bukhara, India, "Chehranamo" and "Parvarish" published in Egypt are also distributed in Persian. Especially under the influence of these newspapers and magazines, which published critical articles about Bukhara, intellectuals changed their views on the reality of the emirate. Sadriddin Aini's words that "naturally, these newspapers... gave more or less new ideas to a part of the population" indicate that these actions are aimed at innovation. It is necessary to assess Aini's scientific and creative heritage not only from the point of view of literature, history, pedagogy or literary studies, but also from the aspect of linguistics. Aini's greatness and incomparableness lies in this - he had the knowledge and the ability to do things that no one else could think of. Ainy knew that he was born for science and creativity, so he devoted all his strength and abilities to the development of science and literature.

One can only admire and learn from the results and achievements achieved by

Ayni in studying, researching and promoting the classical scientific and literary heritage of the East. But it is very difficult to "paw on Aini's paw". That is why his researches dedicated to such geniuses as Rudaki, Ibn Sina, Sa'di, Navai, Bedil retain their scientific value and importance to this day. At this point, we would like to draw attention to some considerations related only to Ayni's art studies. It is known that during the period when Ayni was studying at the madrasa, interest in the works of the great philosopher and poet Mirzo Bedil in Bukhara grew. People of different social classes and different levels played bedilkhan. Poets followed Bedil and wrote verses and takhmis. Ainiy was both an observer and a participant in this process. Bedilga rejected blind imitations as a hopeless creative act. Because Ainy was formed as a clever scholar in the madrasa. Also, an exhibition of his works, the writer's books published in many languages, original manuscripts published in newspapers and magazines of that time was organized in the house. The exhibition includes 8 volumes of books in Uzbek, 15 volumes in Tajik, 6 volumes in Russian, as well as several volumes in Persian and other languages. Sadriddin Ayni's statue, which was on the street for a long time, near Ayni's house, was installed in the yard of the house. Cultural events and creative meetings are also held in this house-museum. Let's take a look at the history of Sadriddin Aini's arrival in Samarkand. Being influenced by the works written by Ahmed Donish, the enlightener born in Bukhara came to the conclusion that it is necessary to open new European-style schools and educate children based on modern curricula. But the emir ruling in Bukhara at that time began to persecute free-thinking enlighteners. During these times, i.e. in 1915-1916, Sadriddin Ainiy hid in Bukhara. On April 9, 1917, during the Jadidist uprising, Ainiy was arrested in Bukhara, punished with 75 lashes and imprisoned. After 2 weeks of treatment at the Kokan hospital, he decided to leave for permanent residence in Samarqad.

When "Ustoz" Sadriddin Ainiy came to Samarkand, he first lived in the houses of friends and relatives. After some time, in 1923, he bought the first part of the house-museum, on the right (the house consists of two parts). In the 1930s, the Government of Uzbekistan built this part of the house, on the left, of brick, based on the project drawn up by Sadriddin Aining himself. "The government created the necessary conditions for the scientist to create," says Farida Narzullayeva. The scholars of Samarkand welcome Ayni's arrival with great joy. Ainiy is actively working with Uzbek and Tajik educators to open new style schools. At that time, Samarkand, the capital of Uzbekistan and Tajikistan, worked in the Tajik publishing house of Ainy Samarkand. In the early days of Soviet power, when Tajikistan was not yet formed, there were forces that denied the existence of Tajiks as a nation. Sadriddin Ainiy puts an end to these debates with his book "Examples of Tajik Literature". He writes this book in Samarkand. For this work, Ainy was one of the first to be awarded the title of Hero of Tajikistan. Ainy's creative room has nothing superfluous - a wooden table, a lamp, a telephone, as well as a bookshelf and a sofa. The exhibition (exposition) of the Memorial Museum is based on the decision of the Government of Uzbekistan to open the Sadriddin Ainy Memorial House-Museum. Sadriddin Aini's rest room is located next to the office. Sadriddin Ainiy lived in this room called "Nakhshinkor" until 1937. Here everything is arranged as it was in the writer's life. In the corner there is a sandal that the writer used to keep warm during the winter, and other household items used by Ainy are also there. In the rest room, Sadriddin Ainiy received foreign guests from different cities. Many parts of Sadriddin Aini's works were written in this room. Next to the porch is the writer's first office, where Sadriddin Ainiy worked from 1923 to 1937.

The stories "Odina", "Kulbabo", "Old School", "The Death of a Usurer", the novels "Dokhunda", "Kullar" were written in this room by Ustoz Ainiy, and the poetry collection "Yodgoriy" was prepared for publication. Here, Sadriddin Ainy met with world-famous writers, heads of state, foreign scientists and scholars: In the hall of the "Nakhshinkor" room, the exposition of Sadriddin Aini's "Life and work in Bukhara" was presented, in which the writer's childhood, his studies in the old school and many madrasas of Bukhara, his friends, and his punishment with 75 lashes, Bukhara it is told that he was thrown into prison, released, and treated at Kogon Hospital. Sadriddin Ainiy worked very efficiently in the new office. Here he wrote the essays "Miss World" and "Historical Holiday" (1939), the poem "Man's Struggle with Water" (1940), the short story "Orphan" (1940), Temurmalik, the hero of the Tajik people, "Muqanna Uprising ", writes historical narratives and "Memoirs" as well as a number of poems, articles, pamphlets, etc. It is known that Sadriddin Ayni lived in this house until the beginning of May 1954. Then he becomes seriously ill and they want to treat him in Dushanbe. Here he lies for two and a half months and dies here. After the February revolution of 1917, struggles for independence began in various cities of Central Asia. Ainy was thrown into prison for fighting against the Emirate. During the years of the October coup, he created inspirational poems and marches in Uzbek and Tajik languages and published them in the collection "Sparks of the Revolution" (1923). In the short story "Executioners of Bukhara" (1922), the writer vividly described the terrible oppression of the emirs and the execution of innocent people with medieval tortures, and in the short story "Odina" (1927) the hard fate and tragic life of the working people. Ainiy's first novel "Slaves" was published in Tashkent in 1934 in Uzbek, and in Dushanbe in Tajik in 1935. The main character of the novel "Slaves" leads to the conclusion that the force that moves history is the people and their loyal children.Covering a certain period of history, this novel realistically reflects the history of the nation, its life and struggle. However, in the description of the years of construction of the collective farm in the last, fifth part of the novel "Slaves", there is no deviation from the dark history. Because the novel exaggerates the positive aspects of the era and exaggerates the collectivization policy of the Soviet government. The main character of the writer's story "Death of a Moneylender" (1937) Qori Ishkamba stands alongside such classic characters as Plyushkin or Gobsek in world literature. During the Second World War, Aini created scientific and artistic works in the spirit of patriotism, such as "March of Revenge", "Muqanna Uprising", "Temur Malik". He also created the work "Seven-Headed Giant" using folk art and folklore works. Among Aini's works created during the post-war recovery, the four-volume "Reminiscences" (1949-1954) stand out. Sadriddin Aini's novels "Esdaliklar", "Death of a usurer", as well as "Dokhunda" and "Slaves" have been translated into Bulgarian, German, Polish, Hungarian, Chinese, French, Romanian, Indian, Czech and other languages. Ainiy conducted extensive scientific research on the history of Uzbek and Tajik literature. His scientific works written about great Central Asian poets and scientists - Rudaki,

Saadi, Ibn Sina, Wasfi, Bedil, Alisher Navoi, Ahmed Donish, etc. are extremely valuable. He was awarded the title of Doctor of Philological Sciences (1948), Professor (1950), Honored Scientist of Tajikistan (1940). Adib was elected an honorary member of the Academy of Sciences of Uzbekistan (1943) and a full member and first president of the Academy of Sciences of Tajikistan (1951-54). For several years, he was a professor of the Samarkand State Medical University named after Alisher Navoi and served as its President from the day of its establishment.

Summary The fact that the traditional local schools, which brought up great thinkers, were completely cut off from world development from the 17th century, stagnation in the education system at the beginning of the 19th century, Hakimkhan Tora, Ahmed Donish. He greatly worried the sages-coaches like Kamil Khorezmi. In their writings, they repeatedly emphasized the need to fundamentally reform existing schools and madrasas. Among the Uzbek thinkers, the first organizers of Usulian Jadid schools were Munavvarqori Abdurashidkhanov, Abdulla Avloni, Mahmudhoja Behbudi, Abduqadir Shakuri, Abduvahid Munzim, Sadriddin Ainiy. Ishak Khan Ibrat and others. This activity of theirs took place in the process of fierce struggles against the persecution and oppression of the governor general, local fanatics, and old-timers. Philanthropic societies, companies, printing houses and libraries, publishing houses established by modern thinkers became a great spiritual and economic helper in the wide spread of modern schools of the Usuli method throughout the country .

Conclusion

In conclusion, we should emphasize that in the history of our country, there are many intellectuals who are enlightened, thirst for knowledge and intend to educate the future generation as well. First of all, they were eager to acquire knowledge, then spread it to the people around them, especially children, improve the educational processes, and create perfect textbooks. They left an indelible mark in the history of our country by showing the right path to young people and urging them to acquire the most advanced knowledge of their time, especially at a time when they were invading our country and looting its wealth. In particular, they left a good legacy in terms of opening a school for children, developing new pedagogical methods and applying them in practice. Because education and upbringing are the real foundation of the future. The political and social changes taking place in the life of the world and our country did not leave the intelligentsia indifferent. They united under one idea and began the work of restoring the spiritual wealth of our people, adopting modern educational programs and applying them to educational processes. The manifestations of this movement went down in history as a Jadidist movement. "Jadidchilik" is based on the word jadid. "Jadid" means "new". The ancients always sought enlightenment. The people's words aimed at awakening are a full proof of these words. Their effective work aimed at reforming this field in terms of education deserves recognition. Of course, education has served as the basis for the awakening of every era. Speaking about the activity of the Jadid, we can see that the activity of the Jadid Sadriddin Aini, who has his own direction and views, is of great importance in this process. Sadriddin Ainiy also sought science and education based on his creative potential. His work in the field of education is of great importance. Therefore, we should appreciate Sadriddin Aini's literary legacy!

REFERENCES

1. Avloniy A. "Tarjimai xol". Tanlangan asarlar. 2-jild. T., "Ma'naviyat", 1998 yil 288- bet.
2. Karimov I.A. "Yuksak ma'naviyat yengilmas kuch". - T. Ma'naviyat, 2008. 125-bet.
3. Karimov I.A. "Yuksak ma'naviyat yengilmas kuch". T., Ma naviyat. 2008. 49-bet.
4. M.Abdurashidxonov, Xotiralarimdan (Jadidchilik tarixidan lavhalar). Sharq, 2001, 109-bet.
5. 8. Begali Qosimov. 'Milliy uyg'onish: Jasorat, Ma'rifat, Fidoiylik'. Toshkent. Ma'naviyat , 2002-yil, 5-bet.
6. Ulug'bek Dolimov "Turkistonda jaded maktablari", Toshkent; 'Universitet'-2006, -B.128
7. Sadriddin Ayniy, 'Tarixi inqilobi Buxoro'-Dushanbe, 1987-C.20
8. Садриддин Айни-маорифпарвар-Душанбе, 2018,-С.7
9. Sadriddin Ayniy tavaludining 145 yilligiga bag'ishlov | Xurshid Davron kutubxonasi https://kh-davron.uz/kutubxona/uzbek/sadriddin-ayniy-145.html
10. Ulug'bek Dolimov "Turkistonda jaded

maktablari", Toshkent; 'Universitet'-2006, -B.128

11. Begali Qosimov. 'Milliy uyg'onish: Jasorat, Ma'rifat, Fidoiylik'. Toshkent. Ma'naviyat , 2002-yil, 15-bet

12. Userbayeva Feruza 'Buxoroda jadidchilik harakatining namoyondalari (Sadriddin Ayniy misolida)'; Buxoro-2024 10-may, -B.437

13. Айни Садриддин. Собрание сочинений. В 6-ти томах. Т.З. Повести, рассказы, стихи. Пер. с тадж. Пер. романа «Рабы» под ред. К. Айни и Т. Гольц. Ред. коллегия: К. С. Айни, И. С. Брагинский и др. Прим. К. Айни. М., «Худож. лит.». М., 1972.

14. Садриддин Айни. Куллиёт/ Ҷилди III «Ғуломон». Нашриёти Давлатии Тоҷикистон. Сталинобод, 1960. 6. Томахин Г. Д. Америка через американизмы. М.: Высш.шк., 1982.

15. l.Karimov L.A. Xavfsizlik va barqaror tariqqiyot yo'lida. -T.: O'zbekiston, 1998. -8.371.

16. Sadriddin Ayniy (1878-1954) | Korporativ veb sayti AK "O'zbekiston havo yo'llari"

17. Дом-музей Садриддина Айни в Самарканде (Узбекистан), поиск и бронирование дешевых отелей в Самарканде https://web.archive.org/web/20180826224147/http://stirringtrip.com/samarkand/dostoprimechateln

osti/dom-muzey_sadriddina_ayni.html
18. Мемориальный дом - музей Садриддина Айни https://samcity.uz/catalog/item/memorialnyj-dom-muzej-sadriddina-ajni
19. 136-летие Садриддина Айни отметили в Самарканде – Газета.uz https://www.gazeta.uz/ru/2014/04/16/ayni/
20. Samarqanddagi Sadriddin Ayniy yodgorlik muzeyida qanday o'zgarishlar kutilmoqda https://oz.sputniknews.uz/amp/20180428/Samarqand-Sadriddin-Ayniy-8082193.html

Literature used

1. SADRIDDIN AYNIY YODGORLIK UY-MUZEYI https://test.samarkandmuseum.uz/uz/site/sadriddin-ayniy-yodgorlik-uy-muzeyi
2. https://cyberleninka.ru/article/n/jadidchilik-harakati
3. https://uz.m.wikipedia.org/wiki/Jadidchilik
4. Jadidchilik harakatining kelib chiqishi – oliymahad.uz
5. https://oliymahad.uz/36485
6. https://daryo.uz/2023/12/11/jadidchilik-turkistonning-umum-harakatidirtoshkentda-xalqaro-jadidchilik-anjumani-otkazilmoqda
7. https://arboblar.uz/uz/people/sadriddin-ajni
8. https://corp.uzairways.com/uz/sadriddin-ayniy-1878-195

1

[1] SADRIDDIN AINI HOUSE MUSEOM

2

[2] SADRIDDIN AINI HOUSE MUSEOM

Sadriddin Ainiy

---

[3] MONUMENT OF SADRIDDIN AINI

F.I.Userbayeva
Chirchik 2024

www.ingramcontent.com/pod-product-compliance
Lightning Source LLC
LaVergne TN
LVHW010438070526
838199LV00066B/6068